THE CHILDREN OF THE GODS

A. B. Curtiss

Library of Congress Cataloging-in-Publication Data
Curtiss, A.B.
        The children of the gods / A.B. Curtiss.
              p.   cm.
        ISBN 0-932529-57-7
        [1. Life—Origin—Poetry]   I. Title
PS3553.U726C45 1995   811'.54 94-74030

Book Design: Cirrus Design, Santa Barbara, CA
Illustrations: All illustrations are authenticated ancient
                pictographs courtesy of Jorge Encisco,
                author of *Design Motifs of Ancient Mexico*
                Dover Publications, Inc., N.Y., N.Y., 1953

First Edition

The Children of the Gods

Dedicated to Dr. Allan W. Anderson
Professor Emeritus of Religious Studies,
San Diego State University, San Diego, California,
no ordinary teacher.

FOREWORD

Some Biographical Notes Concerning the Discovery of the Remarkable Journals Which Tell How the Earth Was Created as an Experiment in Altered Consciousness by Children of Higher Beings.

IN RESPONSE to a request for information about the author, my late grandfather, I offer these biographical notes and a few particulars concerning the discovery of his journals. In 1929, upon his return from an archaeological expedition to the sacred Maya temple of Yaxchilan, deep in the Central American jungle, my grandfather recorded a preternatural vision which "told him" how the world had been created as an experiment in altered consciousness by children of higher beings.

Although the vision occurred over six or seven days, my grandfather spent the next forty years of his life transcribing his original notes into two large journals which have now been published as *The Children of the Gods*. He collected a multitude of ancient pictographs from archaeological diggings, old museums, and libraries which, mysteriously, further informed his writings. Remarkably, some of these drawings, thousands of years old, even depict what seem to be touch-tone phones, computer consoles, and space rockets. There are representations of men in space-suits and pictures resembling microscopic DNA strands and gene splicing which not even my grandfather could have fully appreciated when he found them more than a half-century ago.

I did not know my father's father well. I know he was a charter member of the Appalachian Trail Club and there is a memorial plaque in his honor above the door of a log cabin on Old Rag, a mountain in Virginia that he loved to climb. I know he was a newspaper editor who also achieved modest recognition as an amateur anthropologist, epigrapher and poet.

My grandfather was an entertaining correspondent, especially when he traveled. And he traveled all the time—Africa, China, India. Every month or so we'd receive one of his fat letters, profusely mapped and illustrated. And on his rare visits, he was a grand storyteller with a great flair for the dramatic.

We would have only to ask him some small question during dinner and he would immediately call for the globe to be brought from its customary place by the dining room window. Then he would pull it even closer to the table, clear his throat with great ceremony, and begin his discourse, turning the globe of the world round and round, tapping his finger at each precise spot with enthusiastic flourish.

He told us strange and wonderful stories about the lost civilization of the Maya and his efforts to retrace the steps of John Stephens, the American lawyer and explorer who first discovered the ancient city of Copán in 1839, "Which," my grandfather would intone passionately, "rose up before him like lost Atlantis in the middle of the Honduran jungle."

There would be a stir in my grandfather's voice as he described what he had seen, "Here lie the ruins of a splendid, almost futuristic city, built four thousand years ago by unknown people, employing unknown methods to erect massive pyramids and monumental buildings, impossible to duplicate today, even with our advanced technology. Here lie the remnants of a complex writing and mathematical system, and astrological calendars of remarkable accuracy. The science, the genius of it all! But the builders and the scientists themselves have disappeared without a trace!! Where did they go? Who were they?"

"Some people believe the Maya were survivors from the lost continent of Atlantis," my grandfather told us, and as corroborating evidence produced a paper tracing he himself had made of a pictograph showing a man playing the piano. A pictograph that was made some four thousand years before the piano was even invented!

"Other people," my grandfather said, "claim the Maya were the ten Lost Tribes of Israel or *travelers from outer space.*" He avowed his determination to solve the mystery once and for all, and thus devoted his last years to archaeological excavations and the deciphering of Mayan hieroglyphics.

As to his early family history, my grandfather was raised in a New York City orphanage until he was sixteen and had barely two years of formal schooling. He married in his thirties, but my grandmother died in a freak accident with two of their three children, leaving my father, who was eight, to be raised with the help of a housekeeper, Flossie Luck Farr, an older woman who never married.

At that time, Grandfather was managing editor of *The Providence Journal*, a small New England weekly. When he retired some fifteen years later, he traveled continuously for decades. I once saw a review of a book of his in *Time* magazine, but I don't remember ever seeing the book itself.

Although my grandfather visited infrequently, I have pleasant recollections of a cheerful, energetic man, quite tall, who would wake me before dawn to go hiking, and mimic bird-calls with his black plastic piccolo. I remember clearly his searching, but kindly grey eyes, a soft, brown leather jacket, and his rather jolly white beard. I don't remember hearing that he suffered any illness right up to the time of his death at the age of 94. I never thought to ask any questions about him until after my father died and of course by then there was no one left to ask.

About ten years ago, I received a package with a return address of a Quaker Meeting House in High Gate, Vermont. In the box, carefully arranged in what I later learned were antique embroidered altar cloths, I found what appeared to be my grandfather's last earthly possessions.

There were three books: *Five Acres and Independence,* a worn leather volume of *Robinson Crusoe,* and *Poems of Cabin and Field,* by Paul Laurence Dunbar. There was also a compass; a hand-wrought and much battered silver mug with a dragon handle; a pen-knife; his piccolo; a glass ball wrapped in a black silk scarf; two monogrammed gold cuff-links; a half-dozen old family photos in a red lacquer box; and two large hand-written journals illustrated with ancient pictographs.

There was no other explanation or acknowledgment in the box and I have never been able to discover the person or persons who sent it to me. I put all my grandfather's things together, safely I thought, on the bottom shelf of the corner cabinet in the front hall. I always meant to study them carefully at some later date when I would have the time. Unfortunately and unknown to me, my "self-proclaimed psychic" daughter secretly appropriated my grandfather's "crystal ball" and carted it off to college from where it did not return.

Just recently, my daughter (who is now a clinical psychologist and no longer professes psychic powers) co-wrote a very successful psychology textbook. She mentioned a long-standing fascination with her great-grandfather's journals to her editor. He subsequently read the journals himself, and was so impressed (as he put it, by this "profound original") that he was anxious to see them published.

So, after all these years, I've finally read my grandfather's work for the first time. Now that I have made his acquaintance all over again, I plan to track down his other writings so that I can spend more time in his august company.

R. G. C.
Westport, Connecticut
January 12, 1995

JOURNAL

(October 19, 1929)

PROLOGUE

There were two strange things about my trip to Yaxchilan.
One is that I came to the end of a road.
Not the usual end of the road where there is some land,
    or a house, or another road.
There was simply no beginning of something else beyond it!
I would have said that what I saw ahead was nothing.
But suddenly, there was nothing everywhere and enormous,
    luminous, boundless fullness,
And the shock and surprise of this great cosmic joke upon me
    as I realized . . . but then it was gone.

What was there one instant, in the next was gone.
Gone, as surely as a dream you *know* you've had
    but on awakening can't remember
    though you're sure that it's *just there.*
Gone, though you reach back and back into your mind
You only find some faint fool's gold of memory.

The road turned ordinary once again and I, no wiser to myself
    than hands and feet, regained my ordinary way, the world all
    circumstantially complete and solidly around me.

Since then, however, my eye is not entirely innocent.
Remarkable, isn't it, how the world fits together without a single
    piece missing?

Of the second strange event I've written here at length,
Though the mind remains a mediocre mirror for the truth
    and one is so confined to it.
A child's block has reality that mind cannot encompass.
To see one side,
    the other side
    must disappear.
To contemplate
    the top,
    the bottom's lost.
For reality,
    the heart's
    a better seer.
I endeavor to
    remember that.
But it is still hard, being so confirmed in ancient notions, to sort
    intelligence from knowledge and instructions from emotions.

PART I:

An Archaeological Tour To Guatemala and a Strange Encounter Near the City Of Copán

Only the snakes in the jungle
Guard the city of Copán.
Pyramids that once tracked the stars
    are crumbling in the sand.
A golden scepter
    with a double-headed crocodile
    still clutched by a skeleton king
Taught me
    all I need to know
    of power.

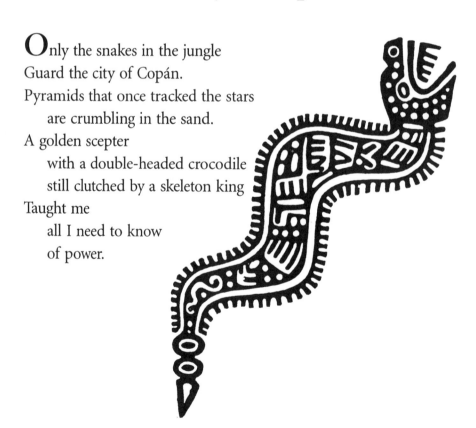

The ancient city was immense (as stories had foretold)
    but dead, and in the shadow of the jungle, cold.
And the story of its people, high-spirited and grand,
    written now in broken pieces cataloged upon the sand.
Why did the ancient Maya disappear? Answers should lie hidden
    here, here in massive pyramids beneath the digger's hand
    re-forming, in cinders brushed from sacrificial altars, dead
    march statues grimacing their warning.

The tour guide spoke of monstrous secrets, tombs of treasure,
    where a sunshine archaeologist might find a summer's pleasure
    in the ancient Mayan ruins.
There is much to study—ritual torture, civil war,
    bloody ceremonies, babies put to sword and flame.
So it was that I, another pilgrim, to this sacred temple came.
To present myself among these ancient bones and learn the
    stories written on the stones.

One broken tablet shows a king, half-naked beneath his feather
    crown, gathering together all the people of the town.
The aura of his arrogance survived the fracture of his frown.
Wild with drugs and ritual anticipation, the king struts forward
    on the dais up above the cheering mob.
Undulating madly, he grabs from underneath his royal loincloth,
    and with vulgar ceremony, slits himself with pointed dagger,
    and twists a piece of hemp into the wound.
Now, almost in swoon, his flaccid bloody faucet flails before
    him like a limp and fraying dog's whip. His man's blood
    flows obscenely down the rope, while he gropes the bloody

13

wick that hangs between his legs, and with this hideous quill
  writes upon a paper bark he straddles on the ground.
The stone crowd screams and writhes, and in a frenzy sets this
  "sacred" bloodstained message to the gods ablaze.
As it burns, the king divines a vision in the smoke and drug-
  thick haze.

A giant serpent rises on its disappearing coils. "What word?
What word?" the tablet king demands. The serpent god will
  answer with the only word he understands. The king lifts up
  his bloody hands and speaks the word.
The word is writ in stone, it's writ behind him and it's writ
  before. It is the word begot the king and made him orator.
The word is WAR!

Small bones show children were abandoned here. They starved
  and lay unburied in the strata. Tabulations from the pollen
  data in the ground show the rainforests had been cut down
  to make room for ravenous, burgeoning over-population that
  grew violent and perverted as their quality of life declined.
What families cannot hold together no ship of state can bind.

Without the trees, floods, drought, and wind erosion doomed
  the land. The few remaining farmers could not fill the cities'
  outstretched hand. First, people grumbled, then they begged,
  and then they plundered one another, thinking to survive.
But violence feeds too often on itself to keep a man alive.
Politics, philosophy, or pyramids will do you little good
If the earth on which you live shall refuse to give you food.

I came to understand it was corruption, greed, and self-
　destruction that laid waste this sumptuous land. These people
　did not perish in their sleep but by their brother's hand.

Did lost Atlantis reach the stars only to find this hell?
Can daisies tell what dangers lie ahead for us, who now live
　well (but for how long)? Here is warning from
　ungovernable violence that these dead did not avert,
And wisdom for a writer, digging in the cavernous dirt,
　in a sun-bleached hat, and a sweat-stained shirt.

But the tour was coming to an end. One more day in the
　desert, then I'd start for home. Do all roads really lead to
　Rome? They must. As surely as we come from, we will turn
　again to dust. It was a melancholy thought. And since it was
　vacation still, for one more day in this sunny land,
I would waste no more of it in auguring the end of man.

I ambled happily toward a near-by village,
Although each step was tolling leisure's knell.
A lazy burro shrugged his dull-toned bell.
A man, materializing out of white hot sand,
　perched upon the sagging porch of his
　relics stand. What's this? An antiquary
　in the desert, way beyond where tourists stop?
I wandered idly through his dusty, cluttered shop. Among the
　piles of ancient tablets, for one who knows the code, is many
　a secret story waiting to be told, of spirit kings and warriors,
　ancestors from the sun, double-stranded helix, talking birds,
　machines that run.

15

The Indian, whose visage seemed as ancient as his wares, watched my rummaging around his store with quizzical and owlish stares. I startled once when he caught me staring back and as he smiled, I, friendly-like, returned his gaze like it didn't faze me. But that wasn't true. Looking in his eyes quite chilled me to the bone. For I did not see his eyes at all but through them, back into my own, as if he wasn't really there.

How could this be?
Tossed from my
    center of reality
    to some vaguely
    distant place and
    back again, nothing
    had changed, but
    nothing seemed the
    same, though solid.
Again I felt that same
    cold fear that comes
    to me sometimes,

The fear that I, alone, am here and all the world is just a dream
    that I made up.
In these moments I seek solace from a friend, listen for some
    sound of traffic, draw the room around me till I'm
    grounded once again. This time there was only this old man.

"Can't find your way back, hyeh?" he said with a kindly rasp.
"So many things here block your path. I can help if you just ask."

"Thank you," I returned, "I'm light-headed.
For a moment I could see nothing. In a
    moment it will pass. Must have been
    blinded by the sun."

"Good!" he laughed. "Now you'll be
    no longer in the dark."

I was insulted by his pun. I made myself all business then,
    browsing through the shelves like any buyer. But of the old
    man's presence I was totally aware. Although he moved out
    of my sight, I sensed that he was there and an energy
    between us filled the space and tensed the air.
I felt pressured into buying some memento.
Anything would do, I didn't much care.

Then I saw a natural crystal ball. I'd never wanted one before,
Not I a gazer into magic things, but letting well and good alone.
This one though had charm for me, the globe had formed
    imperfectly. Pinpoint bubbles swirled like stars inside, the
    illusion of some vast, enormous sky. I bought it without
    knowing why and packed it up and brought it home.

I soon forgot about it as I labored over projects that my
    publisher had planned. There were meetings, schedules
    changed, priorities were reassessed, and deadlines rearranged.

One day while working in my room, I came across the crystal
    ball and set it on a table by the bookcase in the hall.
I noticed how it caught the mid-day sun. Later, in the evening, I
    saw a glowing in the darkened hall, a quite extraordinary sight.

From sitting in the sun, the crystal had absorbed the light, and
was shimmering and shining like a beacon in the night.

I picked it up and noticed that
the crystal was much darker
than before. But within the
frozen galaxy, each pinpoint
star was twinkling, swirling
in that lonely heaven
captured in the glass.

It only lasted for a minute, then
the white lights disappeared.
But for days, each time I closed
my eyes, that tiny universe
appeared. And the strangest
thing of all is that I also saw
the face of that old antiquarian.
He beckoned to me, pointing to the universe that wheeled across
my mind. That strange but friendly sky, that something half-
familiar to my eye.

Then a vision of another place, another time, began to stir my
mind. Where I, a child of strangers, played.
In some dark cave of night I played, and set it all to rhyme.

I held on to the vision, then got paper and a pen and started
writing fast. And fast as I would write, strange words would
come again. Strange words from some strange story that
somehow I knew to tell, line by line and word by word until
the final one.

And then I read, myself amazed at what I'd done. What did I
   write, day after day, night after night? You be the judge of
   that who read these words. Who hear the voices as I
   heard them, curled around my own like vines, whose flowers
   bloom with unexpected and remarkable designs. There is a
   story here for one who has an eye and ear between the lines.

I've heard how ancient manuscripts are found sometimes in
   attics or old caves. All moldered with the ages, pages curled,
   they give illumination to the world. One can imagine now,
   how tenderly those treasures were once carried to some desk,
   assessed, translated, and restored for wisdom's sake.

The greater import was discovered in the words, the greater
   trembling with doubt and fear that doubly bound both mind
   and heart to get the meaning clear. And so I asked myself,
What mystic tome is this I find, not hidden in a cave, but in a
   corner of my mind? It is not here
   by accident. Of this, alone,
   I'm sure. And I am bound to
   it, and to the one who wrote,
   but left no signature.

I do not know these things
   except they were told to me,
   and put me also in some fright
   to set them down exactly right,
And honor do that ancient sage,
   who knows no time and needs
   no written page.

So, thus resolved, I set to work.
Across my mind there came a rush of wild imaginings.
Voices spoke, events revealed their genesis and their
    conclusions.
And what was truth and what were my delusions, I can't say.
When creation speaks with many voices, who can tell where
    credit lies,
Or separate the True Creator from his natural disguise?

Perhaps you'll do the same as I, and simply listen like a
    child who has not learned the judgment of belief.

PART II:

I Take Notes Wildly as an Ancient Journal Begins to Rewrite Itself in My Mind

Regard now this Journal from its creators, and the plans,
    and every importance.
You who listen, remember now, and hear well from the twelve
    who sign our names below.
You will not believe our words, we know.
But in a way, we do not speak to you
    but to the lost self which you have forgotten,
That part of you which always feels alone,
    a little lonesome for some unremembered home.
So listen! Seek you the sailor of your soul,
    for only the wise, who can sort riddle from the rhyme,
    can run before the wind of changes,
    on the journey back from time.
It is a far, far journey that goes not by boat nor cart,
    and never further from you than the reaches of your heart.

So wake up! Be cheerful, and consider all.
We promised we would call whoever stayed too late.
Come! We do not wish to have you wait
    and wandering behind forever. There are other games to play.

Where shall we begin? Perhaps the plot would be the best,
    for if the plot be thick, then all the rest will come from that.
And if the plot be thin, nothing we can say will hold upon itself.
Our words will scatter like the wind, and drift away like sand,
    and dry up like the little streams
    that leave their cracked skin on the land,
    with nobody the wiser for all our clever plan
    and good intentions.
Your own inventions then will have to save you.

So listen to the record and the Journal of our Erthe Experiment.
The Old Ones say that we are children, and cannot know
    the consequences of our game.
Here we do claim credit. (We shall surely suffer all the blame.)
We ask for no exemption for our inexperience.
The right or wrong of what we've done can be only judged
    by that which we become. Our sole apology is curiosity,
And we KNOW that we do risk our soul!

But who can be a god and not at risk? As changelings, living,
    dying and re-born anew, we do provide proof of the
    Changeless, as Truth can only say what *isn't* true.

Our hearts, which have given man his birth in this unique
    experiment, are now quite lost to him, his love, his tears, his
    mirth, and all his problems which can barely be believed!
But the Old Ones have insisted that we let our project go,
    cease to confine ourselves, and leave the laboratory!
They say we have already earned our graduate degree
    with highest prize. We say,
"He does no longer need to sail the sea who falls in love,
    for he does hold the ocean in his eyes."

In short, we are in love with man! The Old Ones do forget
    that gods do not create except from of themselves.
They laugh at us, and say because we're young, we have become
    addicted to our own device. They say we do identify too
    much and lose perspective. They insist we learn the art of
    separation that keeps space between Creator and creation.
We say that distance only leads to disenchantment.
And besides, it is a bore! There must be more to Life!
We will complete the game, and finish our experiment,
    it's magnificent! Already man has taught us *lonely*,
    we would miss his company.

We sought advice from Old Kagami, the Life-transformer
    in the Temple dome. Now they are banned, but long ago the
    ancients of our race planned many. Biokarmic, so they could
    not be destroyed, all were asked to leave and take themselves
    within the time void of the lesser worlds and so not intervene

The Old Ones say that it is all for nothing. "Nothing?" laughed
    Kagami. "The Absolute is always othering Itself to Itself.
Your project simply makes you
    Royal Descendants
    of Divine Continuance
    who write in
    Living Genealogy
    the Likeness of
    Your Own Pretense.

Are we not all come from nothing*
As in the wink of an eye *nowhere* becomes *now here*?"

The Old Ones say we will know fear, and death! "So may you
    hope for courage!" said Kagami.

They say we will be lost, forget ourselves. "So may you hope
    to be reminded in the Word," explained Kagami, "that all
    life is its own one source. Your dreams arise at the very
    center of Existence. Step forward bravely. All Existence is
    your means as well. Dreams don't need anchors, just wings.
If you can *dream* it, you can *do* it. There is no separation from
    Existence. Nothing can be lost, therefore *you* cannot be lost.
God is the most ordinary reality. Where could you go and not be
    in the hand of God?"

What is real can never be unreal, no matter the pretense.
There really is no *in* or *out*, just that you build a fence.
That's true about *beginning* also. The first beginning is not God."

*no thing

There only comes beginning when some end is made.
And there is purpose also only in the end. So it is the end that
will become your birth. Then will come invention and
response. Worlds will emerge from worlds and
consequence each other with authority, reckoning, and force.
Truth, so flung and scattered like the stars, will divide to look
back on Itself like waves upon the sea. So will belief be born
and later trust, and the story of Erthe written by the
children of the gods." We bowed in thanks to Wise Kagami.

We thought it was a great joke on the Old Ones to hide man
in the very place that they
would never think to look,
outside of their belief!
Our days on Erthe will be
the dream to what we
plan while man must sleep.
For then again we will be wakeful at
the source to set the stage. Who knows how man will play it?

There was one who said, "I'll write it down, no matter WHAT
we say. I'll be the scribe to all, miss nothing. But as I am at
the beginning, I must witness, too, the end, and know all
from my heart. I must begin the farthest back and have the
most to go. So, by development, achieve the skill to watch,
and recount what I come to choose. Only thus will memory
regain for me the place device will lose. I will write between
asleep and waking, even to stretch out my hand, write in the
dark, so that the Journal be complete, not wanting any part."

Although I write in scraps that will be lost, misunderstood, and
    turned around, all comes together at the last.
There's something satisfactory in having it writ down.
It is good a journal will be made of our Royal Masquerade.
Are we the first to bring the physical to elevated birth?
Is it not unique, this artistry, this generosity of genius to live
    upon the Erthe as man?

We set up our experiment line by line, for we had long since
    learned to play with time, to move between the planes at
    maximum, to live a hundred million years as one,
To generate morpho-genetic field in intricate concentrics for an
    orthophysic yield.
All this from babyhood
    we knew,
The Royal Wizards
    taught us well.
We have the power
    to travel far,

But there are places power cannot reach. We would know of
    fear, of weakness, and despair. There is much to learn
    from
    prison
    that
    one's
    freedom
    cannot
    teach.

This lesson we would do alone,
The Old Ones are so slow to move
    and we, we would be dancing!
We have drawn lots. One of us will be the
Master of the Game, the First Rememberer.
Though who it is we will not know until the end.
Who draws the shortest bend will be the spinner
    and the only one who can both come and go.
Whatever we forget, the First Rememberer will know.
It is the hardest job of all. The First Rememberer must watch
    each flight, be there to catch us when we fall, and yet not
    interfere unless we call upon him, lest he spoil the game and
    save us from ourselves too soon.

Erthe will become the home of all but one,
    the First Rememberer, who can visit Erthe but may not stay.
For all the rest of us, for all our lives,
    we will become the game
    that we have learned to play.
We'll be the song of Erthe. We'll be the Singers,
    bound to the Erthe by the music that we hear,
    bound to the lives we choose and bound to the shadows
    that complete the small reality that will be all we know.

It shall be written (So one day it may be read): We dare to
    leave our home and all we know and then descend to Erthe
    with all our forces banned to us,
In deep hypnotic sleep, programmed to wake to time alone,
And hear Erthe's music only so we will forget our own.

And as we clip our wings
    for love of sport, so must we die
    to the game to fly once more.
It must be so for the freedom
    of the will
    in which we play our parts.

So some reminder may be needed
    for ourselves, a clue
    in some dark hour when
    we don't know what to do,
When we forget our own true self
    and think the world is Truth.
We may need a bit of insight from a Journal psalm, some word
    to comfort us when trouble comes. It will still come,
    but then to know whereof it comes we can be calm.
    (If we can just believe it.)

The Journal will appear to us in story, picture, rhyme,
Be there throughout all time on Erthe to educate and steady,
Though man, in his unique authority,
    will try to translate what is Truth already.

Come, fellow travelers, and choose your masks in time.
With each a new face for this Special Ball,
    we will not know ourselves at all.
Taking turns in High Disguise,
    we will not recognize ourselves, much less each other!

Who will call, nay,
   who will hear?
We who are born to Erthe
   abandon memory here.

Planet Erthe, Planet Erthe
   on your beautiful ship
   we are coming aboard.
The lines of our dance? Exceeding grace! Our costumes?
Cut to the sword! Our spirit will play in the flowers,
   remember to sing in the grass. Our spirit will rise and fall
   with the hills, will breathe in the winds that pass.

But when we are born to man, what danger shall then befall?
Our spirit, so hidden away from itself, may never remember at all.

Thus does love confuse itself for love, in reckless perch,
That it would send itself, unbound, in its own search,
As any light must risk its going out to gain its birth.

our plan. They *have to do their part*, except for Man.
Man is not bound by nature to do nature any good.
And there were a few of us who questioned if he would.

Man will be somewhat of a wonder in a world of wonderful:
    starlight and sun, snow-flake and soft wind,
      music, beasts, waterfall, and caverns crystalline.
Man, of course, is our masterpiece, the keeper of the garden.
He alone will know that he is there.
All others will not see themselves, they will be unaware.
Man, alone, will know that something grand is going on
    and chase about to find out what it is.
Man, the only bee that stings himself!
The spider spins the mystery of the web.
Man would unravel his instead.

Since a thing divided cannot work as whole
    with such contamination to the soul,
      everywhere there will be contradiction.
One can count on nothing, and not even that.
And man, the only higher consciousness,
    the only chance that we have to remember,
      will be the only thing on Erthe that can forget.
But there's no accident that can befall,
    if one thing's planned, so then is all.
It's just a dance that dance is dancing, yet, born to man,
    we will forget. In that forgetting will our play begin
With all that we have programmed in,
    to learn the taste of fear, the hurt of loss, the joy of gain,

to try and fail, succeed, yet win in vain.
For no sooner will we get our heart's desire,
    then we'll find it is another empty cup we need to fill
    and all we have is at great cost.
Ambition only lives where memory is lost!

And why won't
    man remember,
    shall we therefore
    make him dull?
No, we'll make
    him wonderful!
So intelligent as to
    be left alone,
    how cleverly
    he'll miss,
With no burden but
    excess desire,
    no sin but
    busyness.
Out of nothing* man
    will come.

But nothing shall
    appear to man
    less real than pain, and the anger, envy, lust, and fear
    that prove to man that he is real. Divided from the center,
    nothing works except the middle, which is nothing come
    again. But this is not the nothing man will think he knows.

*no thing

This nothing has no absence and includes it. This nothing
   has no lack and then excludes it.
This nothing is Presence Itself, become a gentle wall which
   holds man safe within,
While he will think himself to be outside it all, a fallen angel,
   but there is no place to fall.
Nothing, to man, will just be the end of the road.
So he will stop at nothing, turn around and run the other way.
And he will keep on running, making episode, touch-and-goed,
   to-and-froed, dominoed, and buffaloed, until he gets the joke.
The answer to infinity will be an open book behind the veil of
   nothing, through which no man will think to look.
Instead, he'll search the
   reaches of the universe
   with sound and scope.
He must look far indeed
   who is himself
   the very end he seeks
   and all its hope!

This, then, shall be the life of man: everything will be
   determined, and the doubt of that, and the degree that you
   try, anyway.
Each man will bear the face of his desire,
   yet think himself ill-fated, far from choice.
He'll cry unto the heavens, "Whyfore, whyfore,"
   with tears and anguished voice.
Everyone will know just what they want and never show it.
Everyone will get just what they ask but never know it.

Each life shall learn from living something carried to the next,
And only by this giving out does something come again, so that
     from each man's learning
      will come light to every man.
For man, the sand will seem
     a part of Erthe, and stones,
     and all the plants.
He'll see the eagle and the
     hawk, though they fly free,
     as much a part of Erthe as
     leaves are of a tree.
But man will see himself,
     alone, not *of* the Erthe
     but *on* it,
Not *part* of the experience
     but working to *survive* it.

The other animals must think
     it queer to see man take to wearing silk
     and varnishing his heels, dividing up the Erthe by names that
     will mean death to change, and following the map of his
     hand, savage unto himself.

Man will forget, then misappropriate the Word.
He'll name the animals and in that naming claim dominion.
But he will go too far and separate himself again with articles.
He won't remember Word is given man
     and not the other way around.

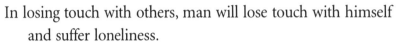

The first naming finds man innocent,
   approaching, full of wonder, awe.
"Thou art Elephant," he whispers,
   in communion with the thing he saw.
But communion soon becomes community
   as *Thou* becomes *a, an,* and *the.*
In losing touch with others, man will lose touch with himself
   and suffer loneliness.

Man shall have what he needs, yet keep so busy after what he
   thinks is missing he will not know it is *himself*, asleep to
   lost divinity.
Man shall have whatever he will ask, unless he *can't believe it.*
   (This shall be proportional.)
To the degree that man does not have trust, he shall resort to
   will. But whatsoever thing he *tries* to have shall by that very
   trying thus be lost, though he will place the fault on effort
   and think to sharp his skill.
(At this one might inquire with nothing wroth, that "We are
   cutting the soup, but can we drink the broth?")

Man's life will be so complicated
   with all its goings out and comings in.
Most men will march the outside, noisy,
   crowded way, and only one who finds
   the quiet path within will hear the
First Rememberer who comes to tell us
   who we are.
For the rest of us, life will come like a feast to the appetite.

There shall be no copying, the urge to continue shall be
      irresistible,
And lack of love shall make the best plot.
All of us are ready now to take a place and invent our own
      becoming.
A skyless cloud descends, the Great Mandala spins.
The dream begins to move us now but I, the scribe, will write
      until the very last.
All will be written, though who knows if it will be read or,
      if read, understood,
As even the artist may later look on the work of his hand with
      strange and disbelieving eyes

The World will be born from the love that we now loose.
We do expand ourselves beyond what has before been done,
      in countless particles of pure Desire to countless galaxies of
      stars from our uncountable Sun. There will be no witness but
      result. Desire's seeds will find their voices, then call forth
      humanity from basest elements. Sense will arise and
      nonsense too. Relationships
      will form, and family.
Society will be complete:
      man, woman, child,
      house, harbor, street.
Enjoy! Enjoy! Life is our
      treat to us and our
      retreat from those
Who seek to keep us from the
      practice of our own divinity.

PROLOGUE TO PART III:

A Chaos of Many and Various Voices Interrupts the Progress of the Journal

Then, like a school-yard at noon, my mind was over-run by a
   raucous crowd of many and various voices rushing to speak
   of their truth.
They sprang right through me to the written page
   as if compelled to leave some marker of their journey,
   some flag upon the mountain of their dreams,
   some precious bit of salvaged love to clothe their naked
   schemes.
I took no calls, I hardly ate.
Their words consumed me, early, late.
All through the day, long into night, on, on I wrote, as still I
   write.

And every time I closed my eyes there was the light and
   then the flight of many voices coming from themselves:
   teaching, explaining, consoling, complaining, succeeding,
   confiding, chattering, sorrowing, believing, denying.

PART III:

Insistent Voices, Anxious to Tell Their Stories, Seize My Mind and Toss It Among Themselves Like a Hapless Bean-bag.

1st Voice:

*As a mother, I shall bare my children to four corners of the
    Erthe, and when they return we shall not know each other.
Yet, if I reach out my hand,
    it will be filled.
I cannot be better
    than doing what I am,
    for who shall divide it
    so that the sinner
    may bow down
    before the saint?"*

The First Rememberer:

*The good news is that nothing is important.
The bad news is that nothing is unimportant."*

2nd Voice:

My child shall be mine as my hand is my hand
    and my hand shall do as I say.
I will show him to my friends.
'Come, see my joy and my heart's darling.'
I shall hold him close and suffer twice
    for each one pain of his.
He's far too fair and fragile for this world's hard
    consequence.
I must decide for him, and save him from all harm.
Oh I do love him so!"

3rd Voice:

As a Father,
    I'll have order in my house.
All things must be paid right.
Not too much on this side,
    not too little there,
Each thing proper-placed.
I am responsible, you know,
    for our security,
    too busy to let go.
I am alone with all this work
    that only I can do.
Oh yes, for love, of course,
Why else would I be here?"

4th Voice:

*Y*ou promised to remember. Go back to the schoolyard
    and remember who was there.
A green coat sits on a vacant swing. A red dress colors the hill.
The merry-go-round runs absently, like a foolish motor for an
    empty world.
Remember me. You promised to remember
    the me who once you were,
    the one who dreamed that you could be."

5th Voice:

*S*ometimes love lies hard and steely,
    deep inside its little half-shell
    where it scarcely bothers me."

6th Voice:

I don't care so much anymore for you to understand me.
If I had a wish, I would wish to better understand myself.
I don't care so much anymore whether or not you love me.
If I had a wish, I would wish to love you better.
But I have sought applause so long
My dancing's stuck to me like glue
And my smile works without me.
Oh, I am truly lost."

7th Voice:

I am afraid of you. You have no space of your own
*   so you eat up all of mine.*
I am like a doughnut to the mouth of your desire.
You devour me, till I'm left hanging on the hole in the middle.
I scream, 'Stop.' But you do not hear.
One more bite and I, too, will be gone,
*   as if I am in the way of your getting to yourself.*
You are a bottomless pit
*   which a sultan's thousand wives could not fill up.*
But there's a crack within
*   for all you will not see it.*
And one day your desire
*   will all seep through*
And you will try to cup it back
*   with both your hands.*
But your fingers will not catch
*   so much as a single drop*
*   to slack your thirst*
*   though you crawl*
*   on your belly in the dust."*

5th Voice:

There are times I'm looking for you, afraid to be alone.
Of course you cannot come, although I know you care.
Sometimes it is like dying for me
To make myself out of something I may dare.
But every time I find myself, you are always there."

8th Voice:

*H*elp! I'm falling into the whirlpool again of a thousand
thinking, sinking thoughts. Uh oh, I'm caught, plunged to the
central core of my despair. Oh, it is rock-bottom here on the
stones on which I break myself. I hate depression, this
horribleness. For lifetimes maybe I have hated it, this prison
of myself where I keep the crazy one locked up, screaming,
screaming, screaming to jump off my mind and splatter sanity.
Well, it's visiting hours now. Throw down the doors to solitary!
I am here to meet my dark, dark self and make a student's study
of my agony. Death, Madness, is that you hiding there?
I don't care. Here, I'll throw you a bone, me. Take what you want.
We can all sit down to the tea of me, us old enemies, we can chat.
Not to negotiate myself. I only wish to visit and know myself at last,
the pain and worst of it, I have no other hope.
I play the wounded hunter here in the jungle of my soul,
hiding in the grass to watch my beasts come down to water.
No drugs now to sleep them off of me. They can drag me under easily.
No? Nobody comes to my darkness here but me? And my pain.
Listen, pain, you beast from Hell, I surrender, do your worst.
I will not whine this time that I be saved (from what, I never knew).
Or do one thing to make this better. I'm going to sit and look at you,
and watch you, pain, like any other show. (Watch for what? Perhaps
I'll never know). Maybe there is no WHAT, but I know this WATCHING
is real. Something is breaking. But it's not my heart. Something is dying.
But there is no part of me that's gone. I am all right. I'm still right here.
It's very quiet. Sober as a shadow now with no adrenalin.
I'm feeling free and nothing's happening. I think the pain has died
instead of me. That's interesting, without the pain, madness is a laugh.
It doesn't bother me at all. Can it be I've birthed myself at last?"

7th Voice:

My y life got healthier when I stopped trying to be right.
Of course I am still tempted, but I stick to being honest
*   since I've learned you can't be both.*
That doesn't mean, necessarily, that things work any better.
But the people all survive!"

6th Voice:

My God,
*   who are we anyway?*
What are we doing that
*   we fear each other so*
*   and hide away*
*   our secret heart,*
*   ashamed?"*

8th Voice:

I learned to extricate myself from the habit of thinking called
*   depression by refusing the VERY LANGUAGE of anxiety.*
Some thoughts are ancient bullies better left ignored.
I put them to the polished sword of my neglect
*   and think instead about the task at hand which, thank God,*
*   continually presents itself. "*

"What do you do?"

"The next thing. Just the next thing. There's always a next thing."

50

First Rememberer:

You cannot forgive anyone
*   because it is not YOU who blames, but your FEAR.*
And besides, you have never been injured.
It is only your NEED, not YOU, that can be hurt."

9th Voice:

*M*y children are grown now.
Now that I have time to read them bedtime stories,
*   help them learn, listen more,*
*   they're no longer laughing out my windows*
*   or tumbling through my door.*
The whole time they were here, I was so busy!
I always said as soon as I was finished we were going to play.
But by the time I learned tomorrow never comes
*   it was already yesterday."*

4th voice:

*T*here is no way to happiness. Happiness is the way.
I think I need to simplify my life. I suffer from too many roads to take,
*   too many cities, too much cake.*
I'd like to find a spot where weeds still grow,
*   I'd like to know the wilderness again,*
*   the silence of a tree, the artlessness of snow.*
I'm looking for an ancient, honest place
*   where they tell time by the clouds."*

3rd Voice:

It's a big surprise. I thought I never would be really happy.
The thing that happened is, one day I just gave up romance and
    wealth and happiness.
I got too old and tired to work for 'em anymore.
So I boarded up my door and sat inside
    with all my pain. Some mornings
    if the hurt didn't come all on
    its own, I'd call it out again.
If hurt was all the friend I was to have
    I meant to claim it good and plain
    and Devil take the hindmost!
That pain, it was unbearable at first,
    but I didn't care.
I suffered out of spite!
Then the pain it started coming tolerable,
    then, comfortable. It spent the night.
Then, visiting was over and it moved home.
I got so used to seeing pain in my best chair
    I got to love the damn thing, fair and square.
And here I am, I'm happy,
    without a lick of happiness, romance or wealth nowhere."

4th Voice:

You can think and think about everything. You can ask
    questions and educate yourself, and in the end,
    you still don't know . . . should you or shouldn't you?"

9th Voice:

What's this I'm throwing away? Nothing much.
Just some old unwanted love. I've saved it all these years.
Now everybody's gone."

8th Voice:

Yesterday I served myself up, equal portions all around.
But when I looked down at my own plate it was empty.
Today I have moved back in, I am taking myself over.
Perhaps I will learn to dance. It's not too late.
I still have a chance,
    a hope, however plain.
Though fear, long
    like a knife runs through,
And the pain of what I should
    have been and have not done,
And may not ever do.
Yet I am here like the trees, to reach out
    and touch the sky with my fingers."

6th Voice:

I think I did something wrong. I don't know why life was so
    hard for me. What seemed like opportunity, as soon as I
    reached out my hand, turned into some divine entrapment to
    betray myself once more.
I feel like I've survived some kind of war.
My children are my medals and my wounds."

6th Voice:

Love is like an eagle on a string. You may as well let it go,
it won't stay tied to the ground."

First Rememberer:

Be cheerful and do some kind of work, even if you don't feel
like it. It is too tiring to lounge and mope at the edge of
your life because there is no rest at night from anything.
That's what makes philosophy exhausting
and chopping wood so splendid.
Dress lightly in your knowledge, suffering, or age,
and go with a friendly step, expecting all good things.
The world is not your enemy, it is your path.
You will struggle in the darkness, but
Your storms have no power over your Sun."

4th Voice:

I am confused. Can you tell me where I started
that this is where I am. And tell me where I'm going
that this
is where
I've been.
Does the man
with glasses
see? And is
the doctor
well?"

5th Voice:

I love you, and I leave you only to become a part of all that
  will comfort you.
So do not look for me in closed places, like a mourner at a
  tomb.
When I leave you, I will be completely free—
  a part of all you are,
  and all you see.
And because I have gone first,
  when you weep,
  even the dust will care
  as I will be caring.
And when your heart is full,
  even the stars will sing
  as I will be singing."

12th Voice:

I'm not saying I forgive you, but I CAN tell you that since hating
  you is painful, I don't think about you much or what you did.
I now choose other thoughts. They say that it will help to be
  forgiving, they say forgiving means to love again.
So I explain that I can't start with you,
I want to make it easy on myself.
Therefore, to trees, the stars at night, new-fallen snow, birds that
  call, and summer rain down-pouring
I send forgiveness soaring!
I suppose to what extent you will become a part of all of these,
You'll also have forgiveness in due time.
But that would be YOUR doing, not so much of mine."

First Rememberer:

Sister, desist, what are you doing?
It's courage, not equality, that makes you free.
You cannot be equal to man for you are his source.
It is you who sends the soldier forth to roam
>   *while you remain his doorway to the Absolute,*
>   *the ordinary way to which the soldier must return*
>   *and bow a reverent salute.*
'She' is just used now and then to decorate the distance 'he'
>   *must come before the two again are one.*
But 'equal', this is simply ugly and cannot be done.
You are the ground for busyness around you,
The chaos swirls around your central calm,
>   *there is no 'More' than that.*
Why would the hub seek to be the tire in motion?
Why would the source of power seek to be the noise of the
>   *explosion?*
If you lose the distance in between the two of you
You both will be forgetting your way back."

First Rememberer:

*N*o man can save mankind. Work hard, but not to change the world.
This whole world exists just to show you to yourself.
Pray, but remember that even in times of despair, the only real
    prayer is gratitude. No problem has ever been solved.
    Problems are just mirrors for your soul, pencil marks put on
    the wall to prove how tall you've grown.
Slow down. Silence is everywhere
    surrounding you. If a little of it
    enters your heart, that is better
    than any answer.
And Fear no failure. The smallest of
    songs is welcome in the world.
And anyway, you are not
    the thing that you are doing or
    trying to be. You are really just
    yourself. To be yourself is to
    be beautiful, for only then is there
    a possibility of Awareness."

7th Voice:

*S*tanding in the corner of my life, I was watching you go
    grandly by on boulevard parade.
I waved a little flag as long as I could see you, until you
    disappeared into the crowd of your success.
The last time, for old time's sake, I stopped by your old address,
    I didn't leave my name.
It's not that you don't live there anymore. It's that you don't exist."

4th Voice:

Is there anything at all I know? Only that I'm here.
Do I even know what place this is? Only that I'm here.
And am I staying very long, or have I been before?
I cannot answer more. Only that I'm here.
What is this pain that breaks my heart?
Where lies the piece of which I'm part?
And when I laugh, or when I cry,
    from first hello to last goodbye, does anybody care?
And still no answer, none at all. Only that I'm here."

5th Voice:

I would give you my song, but my words, like kites, have
    invisible strings that hold them down.
Now, if you could use my soul, that is free.
And you could take it with you wherever you go."

10th Voice:

I can look back now and see
    that I accomplished nothing really.
Plotting and planning illusions,
    like houses moved into
    and out of, and sold,
    and then I moved on.
What is a painted wall, tell me,
That I should congratulate myself?"

4th Voice:

There is no cradle deep enough to rock me, all comfort,
illusion, caused by illusion of pain. And I have long been the
guest of myself
thinking myself to explain.
But I am the music
I dance to, the burden
of my own load.
The path that I travel is
weary and long, for I
am the stone in my road."

11th Voice:

My spine is broken, and my legs are gone. How can I stand it?
Sometimes I can't, but then that passes. I tried despair.
That didn't work. My life came right back out the same way it
went in, just like it is. So I get going, get rained on, laugh.
How else? I don't find myself missing anywhere except in empty
eyes that turn away.
Though maybe not
with you,
I am exactly
continuous
like before
the accident.
Maybe more, because
there's also this depth.
Not that I'd call it a trade."

4th Voice:

I remember young—excess of essence tamed by eventuality.
I remember old—a wiser, kinder creativity. I remember it was
    fear cut out my path, and courage that saved me from it.
I learned late, on a hard road, that problems are all self-inflicted
    and solutions are all self-bestowed,
That it takes courage to be happy, for then you give up any hope
    that someone will be punished for your pain. Not even you."

13th Voice:

I killed eleven people, strangers. I didn't care anything about them.
They found me guilty, I couldn't lie. Now I wait to die myself.
Now I care about the smallest leaf, if only I could see one,
    but there is no window. I've been studying my case,
    looking at the photos; two boys, a girl, one woman, seven men.
I wonder often where they went, and I not far behind them,
    each one, precious,
    the only family
    of the murderer.
The only ones
    who see I have
    awakened
    from my
    darkness,
My beast's skin
    lifeless on the
    dungeon floor.

4th Voice:

I love the winter and the stormy beach, shrieking and cloudy.
The gray waves are so crashing loud, they suck the sound
    from all the people and the birds.
The seagulls mime their flight,
The children, laughing, mime their words.
But I still hear myself calling.
An airy tumbleweed of foam clutches at my chair, then gives up
    to the ruffian wind. They dance away together.
I'm holding on for dear life myself, then I give up to you.
But I still hear myself calling,
Not loud, but deeper than anger, and stronger than hurt,
From far away, where you and the ocean are still one."

11th Voice:

I only learned what love is when I finally finished
    crying for someone to love me.
I remember the very day I gave it up, sunk hopeless to my knees,
    and lacking the face of any enemy,
    surrendered to the only darkness I could name,
    my desperate loneliness.
And I discovered this: Love is the condition of your soul when
    you have died completely to the pain that no one's going to
    save you.
Funny thing is, after that, I realized I could always have
    loved you anytime I wanted, the distance that you put
    between us, being central to your happiness, as beautiful
    to me as exquisite wrapping paper round a gift unopened."

PART IV:

The Journal Describes the Plans for Society.

We will have society most intricate.
So civilized, we'll play at war and wonder why we lose.
So desperate, we'll fight at love and wonder why we're scarred.
Life will be hard. We will not always know the rules.
The SCIENTIST shall take the rules of the game as All,
    and put them together and lean one on the other and form
    himself out of cause and effect.
But the final cause shall hang upon the sky and he will look
    in vain until remembering.

The BUSINESSMAN will be the hook of his desire.
And the ego, that cannot even draw its own breath, will think it
    is in charge. You ask, how can this be? Where comes the
    ego's confidence with lack of knowing so immense?
When nothing can he understand, where comes the self-important
    man, the builder of the cities, the conqueror of the land?
Why, he'll by humbled by the smallest flower, and cowed by
    stars that mock his power. Not so!
Whatever can't be understood shall be called "irrelevance,"
    looked down upon as vain pursuit,
    not useful in the "real world" sense.
Man will be like an architect, who lumps infinity
    along with sonnet, and will not care for either
    since he cannot build a house upon it.
What point to wonder at the moon
    with bill collectors coming soon?
Though God himself be knocking
    at the door, who shall fear God
    who has a creditor?

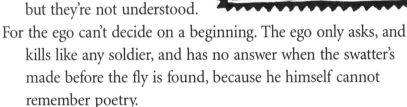

The ENGINEER is like the ego.
He can sort, but creates nothing.
The first form was the circle.
Circles can be reproduced
    but they're not understood.
For the ego can't decide on a beginning. The ego only asks, and
    kills like any soldier, and has no answer when the swatter's
    made before the fly is found, because he himself cannot
    remember poetry.

The LAWYER will be one who lives by facts,
    who did what, and when, or did intend.
He strikes an arbitrary start of things, to prosecute
    or else defend, and therefore arbitrary too, the end,
The lawyer's case the most removed from anything that's real.
The complicated logic needs a start
      and once the start is chosen
      that's the deal, and the cards
      all come from that, no matter
      truth may lie outside the deck.
And the law, the only chance for
    order in the world,
    is merely protocol.
It has no teeth except by vote
And blind it is. For, just as not,
    a sure defeat to one for whom it is their final hope.

There will be machines for men.
The MECHANIC will learn
    everything and then presume to patent it.
Whatever has he made, when each eyelash has been already
    weighed, the greatest of inventions nothing but charade—
A small conceit picked out from the parade by someone who
    grades miracles.

There also come the WRITERS, who fly high with words,
    if only a short way.
Oh, they are murky ones, of such community that live on printed
    pages fed to one another.

The MERCHANT, comfortable, believes his little store and
    counts it over. Like a rosary, he counts with love the things
    his hands have gathered in,
The feel of linen finely made, the joy of silver at his service,
    his friends, collected for their worth.
There is such satisfaction, he's worked hard for all these years.
Who can blame him if some dreams pass by he dare not follow
    when they go by risk of all he has.
He likes to see his bargains safe upon the shelf.
He does not see himself a thing among his things.

Romance, Ah, we have a nice achievement there.
And LOVERS. Here is a dance the closest thing to prayer,
A picnic, wild, and no alarm. And happy the beloved
    when he comes with empty basket
    for as long as that he needs no other lunch but love.

FRIENDS will meet in the park where it is green and free,
Where one can breathe and let fear off its leash a while to run.
What is it, friend, you want from me?
Just company. Just company.

We will play DOCTOR, a serious game for those who don't
    believe that *mind* is a terminal illness.
Sometimes we will believe that we are sick, and the doctors will
    believe that they can cure us of our maladies.
And we will both be right, though they will come to think their
    medicine more real than our disease.
Consider the psychiatrist who will consider you.
He could be right, he could be wrong,
So sorry.
And where is any proof
    except the profit that
    he takes in at the gate?
And then you're told to wait,
    be patient, the only things
    that you already know to do.
You will tell him
    of your problem,
But he won't tell you much.
How safe he plays
    the one-eyed king
As long as all the books
    are on his desk
And you blind to the page
    your pain is on.

The POLITICIAN lives at the end of his gladhand
    and works hard to make himself a necessary.
But man, like a rose, makes a fragile monument.
One hides corruption in its fragrance, the other, in his argument.

The MUSICIAN?
You will
    know him
    by his tears—
Forget the frogs
    in the pool below
    and the dog-eared
    manuscripts.
For what is music
    but the murmurings
    of the spaces
    in between
    when the heart
    breaks
    with love.

The POET cannot kill, though it's not just poetry that comes
    unbidden in the night into that open door.
So let the poet speak what the poet knows, for what is yet to
    come wrapped in his rhyme
    like a miser's gold?
Poetry isn't something
    that you make up
    when you want to.
It's something
    that you write down
    when you're told.

All fame, all wealth, all lovers that exultant sigh
    with ecstasy, just fantasy. A show of fireworks against a
    summer sky and then goodbye.
A fond goodbye, but goodbye nonetheless.

Every trouble that we'll have is just a script that we are
    reading from, a script that earlier was done and we'll
    believe it's real because we won't remember
    who we are.
We will forget that we are not THAT that we have come
    to watch.

But then how could there be a game unless we all believed in
    pain, and anger, love and jealousy, and happiness and misery,
    and one thing more important than the other, the murderer
    who steals our child, the thief who robs our mother?
From where would come excitement? How could we still go on

Unless we thought it was our *lives* we were dependent on?
At some point everybody sees the truth
    that's why we blink our eyes.

But then does nothing come from all of this?
Let whatever come what will. It's we who choose.
And if no one can win, then too, no one can lose.
We do confound ourselves for our own pleasure.
Man is not one night in twice ten million years of measure.
His life is like a phantom bird, whose song is beautiful though
    who knows but
    she sings of hunger
    or alarm.
There is no harm.
We do but play out
    our own game
    that's difficult.
What? You would
    not have it easy?
We might as well
    stay home!

Life is just a lovely place. No more than that, but no less either,
The journey of Awareness through the heart of man.
Thoughts are fences, feelings are gates,
    silence is the pathway back,
    and love is home.
What are we all except the long arm of God,
    the nestling of experience?

There is nothing to be done except to be, for there is no
becoming other than the player that we are.
Which face is not important, just to see ourself, that's all.
It's not that you choose one thing over any other, it is that you
remember who you are, and you no longer care to fix the
dream, but to awaken from it.
Only then our game shall have an end,
at the last trumpet call,
which comes suddenly and out of time.

Until then, we do go on, frantic and faster, frantic and faster,
like a dance of death we think we do alone,
Heedless of the horseman going on ahead, heedless of the
horseman following behind, where every trap looks like the
sole escape from sure destruction.
Until the mind at last gives up its ghosts, and puts away its
fright, and sees that those who lack eternal day
have little need to fear eternal night.

Then Erthe will bring us forth in final birth, and great will be
      the spinning of the wind and fires of stone.
Oceans will heave up, and rush the land with mighty roar,
      turn back upon themselves, and tremble at the broken shore.
Everything that lived and walked on Erthe shall be no more.

Money, like loose pages, will be flying everywhere.
But there will be no looters in this wind. The last object has
      been already bought. The last sinner has already sinned.
It will be too late to change or grieve. Only the love that brought
      us here will go with us when we leave.

In the cities, buildings will now fall, brick teeth knocked from
      their cement jaw. Concrete roads will weave and roar,
      (Even stone oceans break upon some shore).
And as the world disappears in the melting pot, surely it is no
      accident that guns can rust, and lullabies cannot.
Rockets, bombs and uniforms, and other power props paraded as
      defense, are silent now as thieves.
Peace was never possible with these.
Peace is only possible undelegated, in a simple heart,
Not public from a pulpit spitting on the heads below.

Vanity sits on the shelf and gazes at itself no more. On
      seacoasts, rains will pour and melt the ginger bluffs like sugar.
The broken cliffs will slide into the sea like giant fingers
      pointing to the moon, before they sink beneath the waves.
Houses, like raw toothpick staves, will scatter in the wind.

And people will be parted from their purchases with knives of
    understanding when they see the shattered baubles which
    they traded for their lives.

Man! What can he help it, anything that comes or goes?
But he is not to help. In his delight, in his despair
    does man become the instrument of prayer,
    a bit of poetry, and then we all come home.

Man is not forever. Time gives illusion of event,
All from the very first is sent, and only for a moment lent.
Just the little while we're here, we share ourselves with one
    another any way we can.

But there never was a way to *do it right*
And we never were each other's *hers* or *his*.
And nothing ever really happens, everything just *IS.*
Because we have not come for profit but for love
And we have not come to take root but to fly
And we have not come for purpose but for hallelujah!

You who listen, tell the story as you heard it.
 So all know us, and know all by these present:
    Bozart, Phrodite, Desu, Msmra, Vtobn, Lautsu,
    Uddab, Pathagors, Tkespere, Socrats, Cezar,
    Davincheer.

EPILOGUE:

The Vision Ends

There was never any more than that, though I sat at my
    desk long after darkness came, waiting. Then, slowly, I put
    down my pen and straightened all the pages once again.
I didn't pretend I'd heard some holy word, but I surely wrote
    things down I didn't think up. So there was mystery.
There was also doubt and gloom. Was any answer here?
I wrote down words, who knows what more than words they be?
I'd searched the stars, who thinks that stars are seeking me?
Perhaps I had gone mad. Or worse, become a fool!
I'd worked so hard, but my promise, if not dead, was surely
    dying, a bunch of broken memories fighting back the dark.
What should I be trying now?
In despair, I grabbed my old brown leather jacket from the chair,
    and, hatless, dove into the midnight's cold and crystal air.

The world stood quietly, knee-deep in snow.
There were no tracks but mine, to come or go, as I walked up
    the mountain road.
The wind blew, and I noticed for the first time that the wind is
    by itself, and the old owl hooting from its tree, also alone.
As all alone as this stone of Earth I stood upon.

Only the sky seemed companied, glistening in the comfort of
    its countless billion galaxies. Looking up at them, I felt cheer
    for my loneliness, and some forgiveness for the failures of my life.
God knows, how could they be so great and I so small?
Even Eternity, after all, cannot be conclusion so there is always hope.

From some great well of trust my heart began to rise with
    strange anticipation. I stood at the very center of myself.
All the secrets of the universe seemed frozen
    in this single note of time, struck, but not yet sounded,
While I, at the heart of Silence, waited.

And then I *knew*! My nature was my path, it never was my
    enemy. And I have always watched the stars, neither more
    nor less than they're watching me.
Many things that I once had were gone, lost by my own fault,
    or taken from me one way or another. But I still cared
    enough to grieve my losses and shuffle some small dreams.
I have known no darkness so deep it did not have its dawn,
    no hurt so great I could not hear the kindly voice within that
    said, "Get up. Get up. You'll be all right. Keep on. Keep on."

The wind rose up from its
    restlessness and whirled
    the grace of a million
    twinkling stars about my head.
I bowed to my blessing and
    whatever was my fate.
Long, long I stood,
    as still I wait upon this starry hill.
And that is all I know, or ever will.

Sturtevant

26 MADISON AVE.,
SKOWHEGAN, ME.